QUNIANA "AUTHOR Q" FUTRELL PRESENTS

WHY MY MOM
ANTHOLOGY
ANSWERING LIFE'S UNANSWERED QUESTION

Alice Edwards Donna Marie Shanna Thomas
Marcia Ali Amira Michele Ashlie Carpenter
Miss Butterfly Shirlene Bailey Yolanda Myrick
Loneka Ward

Spirit Filled

Why My Mom Anthology
By Quniana Futrell
Published by Spirit Filled Creations
www.SpiritFilledCreations.com

Scriptures marked KJV are taken from the KING JAMES VERSION (KJV): KING JAMES VERSION, public domain. Scriptures marked NIV are taken from the NEW INTERNATIONAL VERSION (NIV): Scripture taken from THE HOLY BIBLE, NEW INTERNATIONAL VERSION ®. Copyright© 1973, 1978, 1984, 2011 by Biblica, Inc.TM. Used by permission of Zondervan. Scriptures marked TM are taken from the THE MESSAGE: THE BIBLE IN CONTEMPORARY ENGLISH (TM): Scripture taken from THE MESSAGE: THE BIBLE IN CONTEMPORARY ENGLISH, copyright©1993, 1994, 1995, 1996, 2000, 2001, 2002. Used by permission of NavPress Publishing Group. Scriptures marked NKJV are taken from the NEW KING JAMES VERSION (NKJV): Scripture taken from the NEW KING JAMES VERSION®. Copyright© 1982 by Thomas Nelson, Inc. Used by permission. All rights reserved.

Michael W. Smith. "Surrounded (Fight My Battles)." iTunes app, ℗ 2017 Rocketown Records/The Fuel Music. Kirk Franklin. "The Storm Is Over Now." iTunes app, ℗ 2007 Zomba Gospel LLC. Rev. Clay Evans. "I've Got A Testimony." Spotify app, ℗ 1995 Meek Records

This anthology reflects the various author's present recollections of experiences over time. Some names and characteristics have been written, some events have been compressed, and some dialogue has been recreated. The advice and strategies found within may not be suitable for every situation. This work is sold with the understanding that neither the author's nor the publisher are held responsible for the results accrued from the advice in this book.

Trade paperback ISBN: 978-0-9653696-5-7

FOREWORD

For many of us, when considering generational or genetic attributes that are connected to a family line; instantly disease and disorders such as diabetes, alcoholism, breast cancer, bipolar disorder, or high blood pressure, just to name a few come to mind. What we don't consider or subscribe to are the overwhelming, yet un-named *issues* that continue to be *taboo* and reoccurring throughout a family line and that's trauma!

Traumatic exposure to events as a child, lays the groundwork to the foundation that's threaded in the mannerisms, behaviors, and responses of these soon to be adults create SHIT, you know that <u>S</u>tuff <u>H</u>idden <u>I</u>n <u>T</u>ightly. This SHIT lays dormant, feeding, festering, and creating debilitating mannerisms and responses, that keeps us stuck. "Hell, we all knew what was going on!" But somewhere in the chaos the message that *they are kids, they don't understand, it's ok, what happens at home stays at home*, and *it's normal* became unstated but very understood.

Assimilated trauma symptoms, language, behaviors, and mannerisms are learned as one of the loudest forms of communication that is transmitted generationally, especially between a mother and her children. This momma trauma series is innovative and nails it, honing in on and creating a window that gives a platform to discuss real issues that are happening to a culture of people. Not a culture to represent a specific race, gender or demographic, but a diverse population of individuals that are linked by a language of trauma!

This language lacks any minimum requirement, prerequisite, specific comprehension level, or socioeconomic stature to learn; the only necessity is the ability to identify and recognize fear, uncertainty, and chaos. Trauma is linked to the most innocent makeup of us as individuals, and that is our senses. Situations in life growing up, creates habits that become social norms, that become a commonality of *it is what it is* or *was* as a way to normalize the SHIT. Remember that.

Trauma is not normal! It shouldn't be *swept under the rug or overlooked conversations that just happened!*

In this momma trauma series, these ladies were able to learn that *pain in life is inevitable, but suffering from it is a choice!* They made a choice to believe that *hurt people, hurt people,* and they discovered empathy for their mothers.

I challenge each of you while reading, don't look at this book as just another one to read and then place it on the shelf. Utilize this tool wisely and pass it on to members of your family. Don't be the only one in your family facing your SHIT, let the healing spread for generations.

Syreeta T. Dawkins, LCSW
CEO/OWNER
Teachable Moments Therapy Group, LLC
http://tmtgllc.com

Trauma Ain't Normal™!

TABLE OF CONTENTS

INTRODUCTION
by QUNIANA FUTRELL

Why My Mom is the unanswered question for many. It was for me. I grew up with a seller and heavy drug user, and felon as a mom. I spent most of my youth and young adult life feeling inadequate for her inadequacies. Does this sound familiar?

Why My Mom is more than an anthology, docuseries, and national movement. #WhyMyMOM was birthed from a deep desire to understand my mom's pain. Honey, let me say, it takes real strength to heal. I had come to a pivotal place where the pain she constantly caused me was affecting my health and mental stability. *Only cowards hide and pretend*, and I was tired of being a coward. So, I did what I had to – I chose me.

Me and women around the world are taking a bold stance and declaring that Trauma Ain't Normal™!

Defined as unresolved drama caused by your mother, many have gone through life believing the lie that *Momma Trauma* is, in fact, normal. Not only is it not normal, but it is also a cycle – and it affects generations to come. But someone has to break it, and I am confident the curse-breaker is *you*.

I do a lot of work for the incarcerated population, and nothing saddens me more than to see a mother behind bars having more peace than a mother who lives in a free world. About 95% of the mothers I assist come from traumatic childhood experience and 70% of their experiences come from not being able to cope with their momma specific trauma. Often, they turn to using drugs, men, women, or a life of crime to numb their pain. Most have the mindset of it is what it is, or I don't care or the ultimate cop-out, I'm fine. When the reality is nothing about momma trauma is okay. A choice has to be made to be *free*. Peace is a choice, and I've learned it comes from within us and not from our environment. *You* have dominion to make the best decision for yourself daily. Choose this day to live in peace- not to rest in peace when you are dead.

The Bible tells us in Proverbs 22:6 (King James Version), *"Train up a child in the way he should go: and when he is old, he will not depart from it."* Improper training causes accidents, injuries, and even death. Growing up with a mother who never dealt with her momma trauma doesn't magically pass on some wicked curse. Instead, she trains you to accept and endure the traumatic behaviors, and when you grow up, you unwillingly pass the same to your children. It is so normalized as natural that we are breeding children, another generation, who learn to accept and repeat toxic and traumatic behaviors. I say, let's have the hard conversations, get help where needed, and start experiencing the life God created for us all. One of abundance, amazing grace, and filled with His peace.

The late Maya Angelou said it best, "Out of the huts of history's shame, I rise. Up from a past, that's rooted in pain, I rise." Champions, it is your time to RISE.

Thank you for supporting the vision of this movement, and I look forward to changing the world with you. As always, "Change the Family, Change the World!"

Quniana Futrell, Ed.S
International Speaker, Published Author and
Philanthropist
CEO of ECE Firm, LLC
www.ecefirm.com

Let's Stay Connected
Facebook, Instagram and Twitter: @authorqfutrell

Trauma Ain't Normal™!

MARCIA ALI

By no means has this been an easy walk through life for me. I've been guilty of neglecting myself on all levels and it has cost me a lot of wasted time. I often feel like I had to fight to finish anything I have set out to do. For example, it took me nineteen years and several unsuccessful attempts to take my nursing boards. However, today I am a licensed nurse by profession. Because of my love for kids, I am a substitute teacher in the Portsmouth Public School system. I am also the founder and CEO of a nonprofit 501(c)(3) named Time Out for Teens (TOFT) and Parenting On Purpose. Both are community-based organizations empowering families. I hope to reach children and parents across the globe to enable them to be great.

My parents separated when I was 12 years old. I don't remember the exact date. I just know my dad gradually faded away. I mean, he was around, but I noticed he didn't sleep at the house anymore. As I think back, I never questioned my dad's love for me because I looked just like him. I have his thick lips, eyes, and a lot of his ways. And no matter what he did or didn't do, I was always a daddy's girl. That's why his leaving me just didn't add up. While Mom never talked bad about my dad, without her even saying it, I could tell by the way she treated me that I reminded her of him every time she looked at me. So, when Dad bounced permanently, it was the beginning of an emotional and physical rollercoaster ride that I was not prepared for, and neither was my mom; She went right into single-woman survival mode, and I was left to figure out life all by myself. I felt like she was too busy caring for my brother to take care of me. My brother was seven years younger than I was. I guess she thought I was old enough to just keep going on with my preteen life without her supervision or input.

To make matters worse, there was always somebody's child, teenager, or young adult living in our house needing help from my parents. I made the best of each situation because I knew people had needs, but damn, why did they have to come to our house? Everybody got attention- except me! The level of rejection I often felt was indescribable. I felt I was unloved and not wanted. By the time I was a full teenager, I was totally wilding out. I became promiscuous and had unprotected sex. I smoked cigarettes and weed, drank alcohol, and hung out late at night, walking the streets of Newark, New Jersey. In retrospect, I was in places I had no business being – and my mom knew it.

One Friday night I missed my curfew well, actually I stayed out all night. So, there I was, walking up to house early the next morning just as my mom pulled into the driveway after working a night shift at the Post Office. I already knew that the situation would not go down well at all. On the spot, I concocted a story in my mind, and I knew it had to be the best story ever. I ripped the buttons off my green corduroy coat and tore my shirt. I was going to tell her that some man kept me against my will and had just let me go that morning. Surely that would be believable. We lived in a three-family home that my dad had purchased for us. On each floor, there was a relative. My maternal grandparents lived on the first floor. My mom, my brother, and I lived on the second floor. My mom's sister and her daughter lived on the third floor, and her son lived in the basement. Usually, Saturday mornings were filled with cartoons and laughter. I had a gut feeling laughter was not in my future. In the back hallway of our house, I stood looking crazy in my torn clothes. My mom saw me then told me to help her bring in the bags of groceries she had in the car. That was not the response I expected from her. I thought surely, she would hug me and cry, then ask me was I ok. Now, I don't remember exactly how the conversation unfolded after our initial moment in the hallway, but I do remember how pissed she was at me. The one who birthed me stared in my direction, and

I saw the pure fire in her eyes. She ⟨
and shouted, "I brought you into this wʊ⸵
take you out." And when I heard her words, I shook to
my core. The next thing I knew, my mom went into her
room and came out with a gun. I didn't even know she
had one, which was probably a good thing. OMG, I
screamed from my gut, thinking my mom had lost her
mind. My grandmother must have heard my screams
because she ran in and rescued me from the wrath of my
mom. I thank God and whoever else that was praying for
me and my fast tale because it could've been another
story being told on these pages, and I would not have
been the author.

My mom is blessed to still be alive at the gracious
age of eighty-one years old. She is still sharp in her
thinking and swift with her tongue. She recently said
that if she outlives me, she's going to write a book about
me. Lol. Currently, I am preparing to relocate my
independent mom from her home. Eventually, I will
more than likely become her primary caretaker. Our lives

as we know it will change for both of us because she's lived in her own home with my brother ever since I moved to Virginia over twenty years ago. I'm hopeful her move will bring us closer. For now, we have agreed to disagree- we are a work in progress. Our relationship is often tense because we are just so different. We process life differently. We think differently. We approach problems differently. We handle people differently. The times that I have prayed for a better relationship with her- I can see my prayers being answered. I know my mom loves me despite our dysfunction. I realize that the affection I craved when I was younger and even now, wasn't something my family showed. Unfortunately for me, I sought it elsewhere. Yup, I was looking for love in all the wrong places. I am grateful that God and time have allowed me to mature in the areas necessary to move forward. Not that I have forgotten the traumatic times, I just found myself a good therapist to help me grow through my pain. Even Mom and Dad have resolved their issues in their relationship, which makes me smile.

They respect each other, and I can share my life with each of them, respectively.

How did I forgive my mom? Whew! Actually, to be more specific, not just my mom, but me, my dad, and everyone else I felt did me wrong. For me, it wasn't the forgiveness that had me stuck. I was stuck because I didn't want to let go of past offenses, and I kept rehearsing my poor decisions. I had embraced the wrong Marcia and tried to categorize myself as normal. Forgiveness came when I recognized what it truly means to forgive. Forgiveness is a daily process for me. Offenses will always come; However, the offense has to be taken for it to take root. Today when I get angry, I try to look at the entire situation for what it truly is. I ask myself questions like – where is this coming from - what is the root cause? Is this person intentionally trying to hurt me? Did I actually do something to upset them? And when the situation is specific to my mom, I ask myself if her anger or words towards me, are they really for someone else and I'm just the closest target. Because there are many times where I believe she doesn't think before she says stuff to me. Knowing the answer allows me to make a healthy choice to pull back, seek God in prayer, and wait for Him to give me direction on how to proceed. Now don't get me wrong I don't always get this right. Sometimes, after all the praying, fasting, thinking, and occasionally over-thinking, I completely mess up. Hey, I am still human. We all let our feelings get the best of us at times. However, I've learned that I have to walk in faith and not my feelings. I have to have a heart willing to forgive at all times. This alone is a full-time job for me because people are fickle. I've always had a lot of mouth, and in the past, when I took a deep breath, more than likely, it was to give me extra oxygen to give someone a piece of my mind. I now consider removing myself or ending a bad phone call so I can think about what I should say. What Marcia wants to say is not always right. I also learned in therapy that if my words are harmful or cause more problems, I need to just shut up. Honey, Jesus, and a good therapist will set you free. Another tool that helped me is listening to a song titled, "A Heart That Forgives" by Kevin LeVar. This song was passed on to me when I was in a very low place, and I keep it on repeat in my YouTube playlist. If you are struggling with forgiving, I encourage you to listen to this song.

To the little girl in me, I say…Hey, Marcia. I know you wanted your parents to stay together, but they can't, and you're gonna have to get used to the house being different. It'll feel strange at first, and you'll probably miss Daddy a lot, but you can get through this. Mom will probably go through more changes before it gets better, but just remember you are strong even when you cry. Sex is for marriage, so don't get tricked out of your panties. You don't have to let boys touch you or disrespect you. That is not real love. Save yourself before you destroy your life. Make good decisions because what you do now will follow you throughout your lifetime. If you don't, people will call you bad names and that my dear is hard to recover from. Learn to love the girl you see in the mirror. You are resilient. You are important, and you matter to God. Your future is so bright.

To the one reading: My momma trauma and my self-imposed trauma went on for decades. There were times when I felt like I wouldn't make it, and sometimes I really didn't want to make it. I know so much about being lonely. I have had to relocate and leave everything and everyone that was familiar to me. When I was depressed and suicidal, I'm so grateful I didn't die in a state of traumatic distress. You can do this thing called life. You can make it, but you have to put in the work yourself. Trust- there will always be people that will talk about you regardless, so make a conscious decision to be the curse breaker in your bloodline. Decide today to address what you know could not only destroy you but also your children. I encourage you to face your hard truths. Make the decision to deal with those things you have stuffed down in the core of your soul. You know the things you've endured that you want to forget about. I have news for you. They are still there underneath all those layers of pain. Learn from me. You cannot conquer what you are not willing to confront.

I know someone willing to help you, 24-7, 365 days a year. Take it all to Jesus, you, and your problems. Take your rest - stop exhausting yourself, spinning around in circles. HE already knows what your struggles are, but He is waiting for you to ask HIM for help. I know you are tired because I was exhausted too in my mind, my body and my spirit. I thought I was in control, and it wore me out. But there was something on the inside of me that refused to die where I was. So, if I, Marcia, can do it, again, so can You. I prayed, I fasted, but I also had to DO THE WORK. If you need therapy, get it because unresolved emotional issues will leave you broken. One day you will come to yourself because you finally got the help you needed. You'll be so happy you did. Let me share this valuable nugget. Your friends are cool, but they are not equipped or licensed to give you clinical help. I speak from experience. Because when you tell folks all your business in a moment of conflict, they will throw it back in your face, disown you and leave without warning. They will cut you off like a light switch and take the light bulb out the fixture too. People are human.

My favorite scripture is Jeremiah 29:11 (NIV), *"For I know the plans I have for you, declares the LORD, plans to prosper you and not to harm you, plans to give you hope and a future."* I pair the scripture with one of my favorite worship songs titled "Fight My Battles" by Michael W. Smith. The song says, "It may look like I'm surrounded, but I'm surrounded by you. This is how I fight my battles." I learned that God is always with me, even when I can't trace him. I fill my house with sticky notes with inspiring messages to myself. For example, one note says, "I matter." I have a chalkboard painted on a wall in my spare bedroom with the words, "I am more than a conqueror, and God loves me." I need these things to reassure myself daily and to speak to me when I can't find the words to encourage myself.

I leave you with a message of hope using a boxing analogy. In the boxing world, when you get knocked out, and the referee counts to ten before you get up - you lose. They call this a TKO (technical knockout). Don't let your momma trauma be the reason you get knocked out simply because you refuse to get up and fight in time. Don't get knocked out because you refuse to train (get the necessary therapy) to complete the process of your healing. You are already a winner. You are a CHAMPION. Now get back in the ring and FIGHT!

I encourage you to consider these questions to begin your journey to being a better you.

1. What critical discussion do you need to have to move forward with your healing? Who do you need to talk to? List their names here:

2. Are you willing to do the work to become whole? Yes or No (there is no middle ground)

3. How has your relationship with your mom affected your parenting?

Trauma Ain't Normal™!

SHIRLENE BAILEY

Associate Minister at Grove Church, Workshop Facilitator, Mentor, Co-Founder of Save the Seed Ministry, Speaker, G. L. Hines Team member; Writer - Marriages /WAOSK Movement *We Are Our Sisters Keepers.* I hope to encourage others with the word of God. To tell the truth, make it understandable, and inspire others along their spiritual journey. After answering the call in 1994, I combined my love for God's people and enthusiasm to teach and serve at every opportunity given. Continuing in my call, I joined G. L. Hines Ministry as a writer focusing on marriage. As a Pre-Marital Facilitator, I help women explore, *the role of the wife.* Proudly served 19 years as Co-founders of Save the Seed Ministry inspired by the Mamie Till, mentoring girls 8 – 18. I'm the mother of five adult children, 13 grandchildren, and have been married 37 years to Gary E. Bailey Sr. After suffering an injury, I found myself in a holding pattern, especially concerning ministry. As I struggled to find a new normal while remaining faithful to the call, I sought God for direction. I heard "it's time to write." I obeyed God's instruction being faithful, knowing it will be the key to someone's deliverance.

My mother was a great mom, a superhero, if you would. But kryptonite called alcohol often debilitated my superhero. Mom worked hard, went to school, and earned two college degrees while raising four daughters on her own. Her struggle was real. It would be her love for her high school sweetheart, my father, and the love of her life where it all began. My father was a very talented musician, a singer, and a highly intelligent man; however, he lived out his life as a heroin addict, incarcerated for most of their marriage, and absent most of my childhood. As I reflect, words cannot express the things we experienced because of his addiction. Years of broken promises and shattered dreams, which I believe were directly linked to her alcoholism. Yes, it was my father, a broken man who broke my good mom.

At nine years old, I remember coming in from school; mom had been called from work and had entered our home only to find strangers that were foaming at the mouths, needles hanging in arms; some were near-death and their bodies convulsing; it was a drug party gone wrong. Everyone had shot up from the same bad batch. Sirens blaring as EMTs, firefighters, and police worked to save lives. Pandemonium had erupted. This episode and many more over time weakened the resolve of my mom. It was an almost certainty following an incident like this that Mom would be found at Mrs. Nanny's speakeasy, drinking her problems away or so she thought.

Early in life, watching mom, I despised alcoholism and its effects, vowing never to drink. Even though I kept that vow, the dysfunction of alcoholism still found its way into my life. I struggled almost daily in my youth and young adult life. I became indecisive, insecure, fearful, and suffered from low self-esteem. These flaws contributed to my compulsive behaviors of binge shopping and as harmless as it may seem an addiction to chocolate. As a mom, I, too, used things to anesthetize my pain. Initially, I didn't make the connections because they seemed innocent enough; However, the destructive nature though subtle was still a stronghold I needed to break. The effects were both positives and negatives in my life, a life I'd settle for until I realized that trauma was not normal.

My mom's binge drinking brought together two colliding worlds; one was secure, orderly, and wholesome, while the other was the opposite. The uncertainty of these addictions caused me considerable difficulty as I struggled to navigate between these two worlds effectively. Her addiction, and depression which fueled suicidal thoughts, along with the victimization she suffered, left me feeling like women were helpless beings, especially those who drank. I hated alcohol. Whenever there was any family gathering, I cringed, sick in my stomach wondering, hoping, and praying that there would be no liquor. I was so traumatized it sobered me for life.

I was a child yet, older than my years, afraid but bolder than my fears, fragmented but whole enough to fight, why? Because even in her brokenness, my good mom, my superhero taught me how to survive despite the fragmented pieces in her own life. Even in her drunkenness she cried aloud to God in prayer.

Hear my cry God; listen to my prayers, from the ends of the Earth I cry unto THEE, when my heart is overwhelmed (grows faint inside of me) lead me to the Rock (a place higher then where I am). Psalms 61:1-3 (NKJV)

I encourage you to strive for healing from your momma trauma; to find the good things. Even if it comes down to your mother merely giving birth and bringing you into the world. I vividly remember a good thing. As a child, I was looking up at the night sky, seeing stars as I went in and out of a Grand Mal seizure. Hearing feet pounding the pavement, my mom ran frantically with me in her arms to the nearest hospital for help. Sitting by my bedside, I awakened to find her in a nightgown shaking, crying, and praying for me. Later, the nurses gave her a hospital robe to cover herself, then pulled together enough cab fare so she could get back home. These women praised her for the motherly love she displayed. Even with the faint smell of alcohol on her breath, I will never forget that night when my mom ran barefoot, in night clothes with no reservations to get me help. Overwhelmingly, I felt her unconditional love for me. The following Sunday, mom took us to church. She had convinced herself that a few squirts of perfume and some Wrigley's gum would keep her secret. She approached the Elders of the church, and laying me on the church's altar asked for a prayer of healing. My super mom, my good mom with a bad habit, gave me so many moments that served as the good things I knew about her despite her addiction.

Years had passed since my mom had taken a drink; however, every now and again, she'd have to pass my lingering suspicions test. There was still a part of me that expected the resurfacing of good Mom's bad habit. I mean, it had done so many times before. I had forgiven her but I did not allow Mom to forget the effects of her alcoholism on me and, subsequently, my children as well. This behavior threatened my healing. Although I realized that none of her actions was done to hurt us, my sisters and I, could not move on. Our traumas need for validation overrode our forgiveness. We didn't understand why she couldn't see how her alcoholism was, in part, a direct link to the dysfunctional behaviors we displayed in our lives or the trauma we had suffered as a result.

As damaging as it was, she believed the trauma of her alcoholism only affected her, so my good mom, who had a bad habit, had to face the gut-wrenching truth, that we, in fact, had been traumatized. That it had affected us in many ways. We were young women perplexed at how we could be both strong and fragile, self-sufficient yet needy, confident but approval-seeking, and brave enough to face the challenges of life while fearful of any sign of rejection. Forgiveness was the only option, but we couldn't, no we wouldn't allow this now transformed, delivered mother and grandmother forget. We forgave but not without repeating the story, reliving the pain, and inadvertently punishing ourselves and causing Mom to live her shame again. One day with tear-filled eyes, my mom said, "My grandchildren don't know that woman. I have not been that woman for years." The residual of our trauma still kept resurfacing and contaminating our relationship with each other.

When my mother passed away in May 2011 from stage four lung cancer, I'm happy to reveal that our relationship was in a good place. I thank God for bringing us through the process of forgiveness, and I thanked my mom for forgiving me for the thoughts, feelings, and judgments I held over her. I truly miss her so very much. When she passed, I had peace because the question of forgiveness had been faced head-on – I had forgiven her. Truthfully sometimes the process felt like rough rocky patches, with jagged-edged slopes that left both our egos battered and bruised. However, we gave validation to one another's traumas. I had to acknowledge momma had trauma, too, and the cycles in my life had to be broken. I thanked God for forgiving me for the disgruntled thoughts of why my mom or why ME. The thoughts we think but are too fearful of saying aloud. Then it happened. I understood I had to forgive myself. I had to take ownership of my role in our relationship, every feeling, every thought, word, and or action in order to heal.

God forgave us, and He has instructed us to forgive one another. Forgiveness is a Godly Principle. For us to begin the process, we must forgive. But it doesn't stop there; we must work at it. I read a quote once that said, "The hardest thing to give; is to give in." anonymous

It baffles me how quickly we forgive others but aren't so willing to show the same forgiveness to those closest to us. When we truly love someone, forgiveness should be our only option. The process may be difficult, but we must keep in mind that it is both a Godly principle and a discipline to walk in forgiveness. So, don't keep treading on the wheel of condemnation, accusation, or rumination, mulling over the idea, again and again, just forgive!

Sometimes I reflect on what my sisters and I have been through; How dysfunctional behaviors, generational curses, and traumatic experiences brought on some great battles, and I just break out in praise, giving God thanks for what He brought us through. I'm so grateful for God's grace and Mom's prayers. She regularly attended church with her grandmother. During her recovery period, she would fondly recall the prayers of her grandmother. She recognized it was God's unconditional love that rescued her from a life of shame and self-destructive behaviors.

How am I alive? How did I forgive? How can I love? The answer is, it was all made possible by Christ, who gives me the strength to overcome. I do so with daily prayer and practical applications. I learned to put God's words into action. So, if you're still wrestling with the pain of the little girl inside you, put your big girl pants on, and work to overcome the effects of your trauma. I encourage you, don't give up. Keep the faith; it's a process, but it's doable. You can do it. There is light at the end of the tunnel. Believe me, when I say, little girls grow-up. When the pain no longer paralyzes you, you will be ready to tell your story and confront your momma trauma. Maturing physically and spiritually opens your understanding that momma had trauma too; she was trying to COPE (Carrying Our Problems Externally), with the internal pain. When God revealed my need for inner healing, things previously used externally became non-effective.

Sister friend, you can overcome the residual effects of dysfunctions or inherited generational curses. You may have inadvertently learned behaviors associated with addictions, such as self-destruction, sabotage, or strongholds that have kept you bound, but today is your day of reckoning. Ask yourself, "Do you want to be healed? Do you want to be delivered? Can you live victoriously?"

My friend, you can be healed, especially as believers. You now have heavenly DNA at work in you. A Father who can and will help you overcome all things. So, if you're reading this and you're now a mom struggling with life issues and like your mom have used external means to anesthetize an internal pain. You're living a life that replicates your mom's, and like Elle Varner, you ask, "Can I get a refill?" To swallow your pain, I challenge you today to be brave, get help, and get healed. You know the damage it caused you and the potential damage it can cause your children. Give them a chance to be whole and healed.

Sister Friend - like the woman with the issue of blood, you've been bleeding out for some time now, but there's good news, your healing is just a decision away. You must press to touch the hem of His garment. You can do it. Many have witnessed the stains of your issue, but it's not too late. Seek God on the matter. Get an accountability partner who will check you in love. Depending on your level of dependency or addiction, you may have to seek professional counseling. I encourage you to seek help through your local churches, such as Restoration & Recovery Ministries. Find a reputable support group of women who will walk you through and out of your dysfunction. Last, put into practice daily applications that will aid in your healing process. When I did, I looked with new eyes at my mom's story. Looking at the people and things that shaped her then, I understood that my good mom with a *bad habit*, and my superhero, only gave what was given to her. With great confidence, I genuinely understand she gave and did her very BEST.

TRAUMA AIN'T NORMAL

Miss R Brittany Ruly

Life long
Friend love
you so much
Thanks for always being
there!
Tray

MISS BUTTERFLY

As a prior felon, I am now the proud owner of my Nail Salon, called OnSite Nails (www.onsitenails.com). I pride myself on being a special type of Nail technician. I love to create beautiful nails and fix the feet of those who never thought they could show them in public. I keep men detailed and women classy.

Who in the hell is my mom? I still don't know.

The drama my mama gave infected my life deeply like a disease. I feel like I have been a source of cancer to her from the moment I was born in her tubes and came out weighing only four pounds. It's like she feels I ruined and endangered her life with my life. I'm surprised I even got here having a sperm donor (dad) who was and still is mentally ill. I have a lot of bad memories in my head from those two. But what I most remember were the ass whooping's she and I got from him, and the multiple times he tried and failed to kill me, her and his self.

From a young age, I was left to raise myself because my mom was a workaholic. I never really saw her much as a child. I had an older sister, but she was too busy living her own life and shut me out a lot. I think I was an ordinary girl until I turned eleven. Then, I learned the streets quickly. By the time I was 16, I had been raped and would soon become a teen mom. I was six months along when I found out that I was pregnant, and my mom 'bout lost it on me. I can still feel her heavy open-handed slap to my face in broad daylight, right down the street from a police station. She was so pissed and angry. But I don't think her anger was all on me – I really think it was because her married boyfriend at the time left her; His sorry ass wanted me to get an abortion, but I am so glad I didn't. I want to say that was my last time disappointing my mama, but it wasn't.

My mom and grandmother, both of them, are crazy superstitious. My grandmother, who was a full Indian, believed that for every good day, two bad days were coming behind it. Mom believed too much laughter and fun was disrespectful and would bring a life filled with tears. Which is what happened to her the day my grandfather, her daddy, died. My cousins, sister, and I were laughing and playing in the front room when Mom got the call about his death. When she hung up the phone, she came screaming into the room, "You killed him, you killed my daddy!" Imagine me playing and having fun one minute and then being blamed by her of killing a grown man in the next. But in her world, I had killed him. In reality, my grandfather died from diabetes, but 'till this day, she blamed me for it. Again, it was just another example of why I couldn't satisfy her as a daughter. Maybe that's the reason my momma pimped me out to older men when I got older. I can still smell the scent of that husky lotion they rubbed all over my body. I wonder how much money she got?

Some say we look for love in all the wrong places, and looking back, I see why my outlook on life was so different. I searched – for a mom, for attention and any kind of affection. I called other women mom, some I knew well, and some I didn't, because I wanted a real hug, kiss, or a mother talk. Maybe that's why, for a time, I was a lesbian.

I still have, to this day, a void. I think a part of me still hopes my mom will step up and want a real relationship with me before she dies.

Now don't get me wrong, my mom has financially taken care of my daughter and me, and we will never forget it because that's all we hear about is money,

money, money. I have never seen someone that needed so much money in my life. For the record, let me say, paying someone's way is not love. Money and things do not make everybody happy. There were times in my life that I thought I had to buy things in order to make my mom happy, or like me, or love me. And as I grew up and matured, I decided, either way; She would take me for who I was, or that's that- I refuse to buy nothing or nobody – even my mom. When I give her money, she loves me. But when the money is gone, she hates me. I've never seen anything like it in my life, but I live it every day. What kind of parenting is that? And when I call her on the carpet for it, she says, "What did I do wrong?" One day I'm going to answer her truthfully and say, "Everything. You did everything wrong!"

My mom is still living, barely. She has kidney failure and severe diabetes. As of now, I live in her household, and I am her full-time caregiver. We can't get along for even a day. I'm sure it's because we don't talk about the things we should talk about. Even now, her love is still expensive. I wonder if what's between us is really love or do I got to pay her for love? At times I don't know what the answer is.

Forgiveness is here, and I do forgive my mom, but I will never forget the things she's done and said to me. I try to keep my heart pure and listen to God when He speaks to me. I hear God's voice, whispering, "She needs help, your help." I know hurt people hurt people- that I understand and have made peace with it. But when it comes to my relationship with my children, I will go about my parenting a whole 'nother way.

To the little girl in me, I'd say, Hey Shay-Shay, you are loved, and you will be someone very special. I'd tell her, look in the mirror, you are beautiful and girl you got it go'in on. Your weight and size do not define you or your future. Get with yourself and cherish your heart. Be cautious of who you let in, and be careful who you let out. Everyone is not designed to sit on the front row of your life with you. Times will get rough but learn who you are before you go looking for something or someone you'll regret later. Money isn't everything and child, you can't buy happiness. And forgive momma. She's in denial about a lot of issues in her life, of which you had nothing to do with.

To the one who is reading my story: Hey, what's wrong with you? Turn around and look how far you've gotten. Now turn back around and look forward- it's not over, keep going. Remember "Nobody can hurt me (you) without my permission." – Mahatma Gandhi.

I believe I'm alive solely to witness to you. Use my life, the good and bad, as a witness. I've been through some unbearable things, but today I'm an overcomer, and so are YOU.

Let me further encourage you by suggesting you listen to this song – it is everything - *No Battle, No Blessing* by Shari Addison. Hey Champ, I'm singing to you –"it's over now. It's over now, I feel like we can make it, the storm is over now." That's true, honey. I bet you thought life was over and done. You were ready to die and give up, but that fighter in you keeps punching and kicking. Guess what? You've won. Always know that it was hard getting through the fight, but I'm so happy you never gave up.

Question 1. Do you know who you really are? Have you tapped into your potential?

Question 2. Do you have a plan to make a difference in your children's lives? If you don't have any children- how do you plan to make a difference in your life for the people that depend on you?

Question 3. Ever thought of getting a mentor? If not, do it. We all need someone to show us the way.

Trauma Ain't Normal™!

ASHLIE CARPENTER

Also known as Ms4ft11. I am from Chesapeake, VA. Having been diagnosed as a child with an IEP, I never truly thought I would become a winning woman of authority, influence, and valor. My story is a true testament of going through the fire and being refined by God. Being refined took me from public assistance to feeling like a loser. By 2006, I had had enough. By the grace of God, I finally tapped into my power and worked my way off public assistance - as a single mother. I am now a full-time M.O.M. (Multiple Occupational Manager). Yes, your girl is a full-time entrepreneur, owner of Ms4ft11 LLC Sweet, Speaks, Support – where our products are sweet treats, and our mission is to win in life. Besides keeping my house in order, I have three amazing kids involved in many activities. I am a professional cook, a public speaker, and a virtual assistant. I also support my creative husband, Robert, in his multiple business empires.

Craving my mother's love didn't stop me.

I was raised in a single-family home where my mom taught me that love came from my grandparents, not my parents. As I look back, my mom was an excellent provider. She made so many sacrifices throughout my childhood so that I could go on trips, shopping at the mall, and so much more. I had all the stuff that I wanted but nothing of what I needed. Instead of shoes and clothing, what I longed for was a hug, a kiss or the words "I am proud of you," or even "I love you."

I know my mom was forced to have me at 15; her family did not allow the termination of a fetus. But when my mom got older, she didn't think like her parents because when I got pregnant at 16, abortion was the only option she forced upon me. I wonder if her situation was reversed would I even be here today. Again, all I ever wanted from my mom was love, but what I felt was rejected and not being unwanted. It seemed to me that the only time I brought her any joy was when she found out I had a learning disability.

As a child in elementary school, I struggled with reading and writing. Those subjects did not come easy for me, so I was tested, then labeled LD (learning disabled) and given an IEP. That day it was as if my mom said, "oh, she's slow." She never said those words aloud, but she made me feel like she wanted to - like the IEP was her stamp of approval. Since she nor anyone else explained to me what an IEP was, I assumed there was something wrong with me. Especially in school. There were so many kids that said mean things regarding the kids in the special class, and once I was a part of that special group, I viewed myself the way they saw me. In my eyes, I was the dumbest child in the world and that I could never do what other kids did. But what my mom would later say to me impacted me far more than what the normal kids in school said about me.

I do not know what I did or said, but I was around seven or eight years old when I made her angry enough to tell me, "If I didn't have you, I would have my car and my house." Her words of regret stung and wounded me.

Fear gripped me so hard, that even as an adult, I still deal with feelings and thoughts of not being the child she wanted. And for the life of me, I didn't know what or who I had to become for her to receive me as her own. So, I began to search – for a mother. I sought and clung to women that I hoped would satisfy my heart's cry. Unfortunately, they too hurt me in some shape or form, and I was faced with reality. I already had a mom.

But years of negative self-talk, low self-esteem and rejection issues prevented me from even giving my mom the chance to know the real me. I had built up so many emotional walls and refused to show her my true potential. I showed her parts of me but never the full me – the speaker, financial coach, and writer. I had convinced myself that the only thing that I did to make my mom proud was my IEP. And that lie held me bound. But I'm not dumb. And for anyone who may have been diagnosed or knows of anyone who has an IEP designation, an IEP is help and nothing more or nothing less.

My mom is alive and well, and we are becoming great friends. We talk almost every day, and yet there is still a piece of me that craves her acceptance. I want to hear her say, "Ashlie, you're doing a good job in life. I'm proud of the woman you've become." There is progress like when she says, "Much love." But it's never a full, "I Love You." To be honest and even more transparent, I'm afraid to ask her why she can't or won't wholeheartedly say the most powerful three words on the planet. However, I have learned to focus on the positive, and this past Mother's Day, she kissed me for what I believe to be her very first time doing so. It was the best feeling ever!

Like the song says, "When I look back over my life and think things over, I can truly say that I am blessed, I have a testimony!" I know that I know I am still alive only by the grace of God. I remember the times I took pills trying to take my life because I was convinced I was too stupid to have a purpose. I also knew that my mother and I would never get along and understand one another

— that my life would be a living hell. I prayed not to wake up, and when I did, I was so upset. I wanted to tell her what I had done, but I was too afraid that when I did, that would only make her even more upset at the fact that I had been born. But God! I was raised in the church, but I did not have a relationship with Jesus for myself. All of that changed after I got pregnant with my daughter. I knew then that I would need God more than ever. God held my hand and transformed my life for the better. Even when I foolishly tried to walk away from him, God kept calling my name. So truly, it's the grace of God that keeps me alive.

If I could give the little girl in me a message it would be, it will all work out for your good. The trauma, your mama, all of it. You are more than enough just as you are — all smiles, silly, and with an IEP. Yes, you learn differently, but that does not make you less than anyone. So be all that you want to be. Follow your dreams of getting that degree in social science, followed by becoming a psychologist. Yes, you may have to work harder than your peers, but do it anyway. You got this.

I have genuinely forgiven my mom because I know she only gave me what she was taught to give. I do not blame her, now, for anything she said or did to me. Forgiveness has made me strong. If it weren't for my negative experiences, I wouldn't be as careful and intentional with my word choices as I am, especially with my kids and others. Words, our words have power!

This journey to heart healing helped me understand that it is okay to ask for help. As a married adult with children of my own, I was still a little girl crying out for my mother's love. I found that prayer worked, but I needed more – a specialist in my specific kind of trauma. I wanted to be whole in my emotions. Not only did I find a therapist, but I found a bible believing therapist - look at God. He will honestly give us what is needed. So, get help and do not let anyone talk you out of it. In most communities, especially African-American ones, therapists are looked upon as people who help crazy folks. That is only partly true. They also help people like you and me to process and move past different kinds of trauma like death, war, and even momma trauma.

To prepare for the writing of this book, I had a talk with my mom and aunt about mom's statement. Mom said she didn't remember saying it, and if she said it, she was drunk. My aunt said at the time, my mom was depressed and wasn't doing well in her relationships. Does that make it right? No, it does not. And therapy made me realize that I wanted an earnest apology from my mother – and it was okay to want that.

If you need help, please ask for it. It saved me.

My favorite scripture is Luke 1:45 (KJV), *"And blessed is she that believed: for there shall be a performance of those things which were told her from the Lord."* In this scripture, Mary was told she would have a child, and that specific child would save the entire world. And Mary was chosen to be the keeper of such greatness, and she believed just that. I had to believe the same for myself. I am a keeper of greatness, and just as Mary had to share with the world, I believe God wants me to do the same. I believe every blessing from Genesis to Revelation is also a blessing for me. There shall be a performance of God's Word for me!

To the reader: I speak right now, not only will you have a breakthrough in your relationship with your mom, but you will also begin the journey to healing. You will have such a peace fall on you to know that you are enough. You mean so much to God that He placed this book in your hands. God wants you whole, with nothing missing and nothing lacking in your life. I speak that the boldness and confidence of God will find its way into your heart so you can ask for help and not feel ashamed. Today, you will shake off the past and live life to its fullest potential. You will be all God called you to be. You will fulfill your purpose. Today will be different. Today you will win.

As you answer these questions, I want you to remember you are enough, and you matter.

What has stopped you from getting help? Is it people's opinions?

How long will you decide to stay in the hurt?

If you get the help and healing you need, would it help someone else?

Trauma Ain't Normal™!

ALICE EDWARDS

I am a pediatric nurse. I aspire to be an advocate for the little voices, a nurturing soul for children in need, and a teacher for the moms who want to know how to get this thing we call life, right.

I've heard the mantra, trauma ain't normal, and I say to myself, *yes, it is; at least in my world, it feels like it.*

I grew up in trauma. My norm was trauma. My mom was and still is a drug addict. Literally, for my entire life, she's lied, cheated, and has stolen from me, her only child. That means for over 13,030 days, my mom has been on drugs. Often, I've had to move in and out of state. They took away me from family and friends all because of her flings and so-called modeling career. What has impacted me the most is knowing the fact that she doesn't believe there is anything wrong with her. And what I wrestle with emotionally is I have her full name. Am I really supposed to continue her legacy? I live my life in paranoia, constantly thinking about how not to become her and how not to abandon her. Because no matter how bad she gets, I am all she has. But there is a deep, even protective part of me that takes precedence over my mom. I cannot allow her baggage and addiction to damage my children the way she's damaged me. I still hide things in my home. I prefer not to carry cash in fear that it'll be stolen. I even watch people around me thinking, *are they on drugs too?*

However, there is one good trait I got from my mom, and it's the discipline of consistency. Although life has been challenging for me, and I have desired to throw in the towel, I have not. I've consistently refused to receive the spirit of death when it kept knocking at my door. I still choose to live because I dogmatically refuse to be another statistic. Just a number with no kind of destiny or purpose. Another black woman who fell to the pressures of life and didn't make it. Another poor little girl who had a rough life and couldn't handle it, NO! I made a promise to myself that I would not allow my children to feel the embarrassment or loneliness that comes with an addictive parent. I promised myself, and I pray to God every day to grant me the wisdom and strength needed not to allow me to cause that type of pain and mental hurt to my children. I *will* be the parent my children can count on- not look for.

I'm grateful my mom is still alive. But my heart aches because she is still an addict. Our relationship has a different dynamic now. She makes a better effort to hide her tendencies when we are together. We see each other with no particular consistent pattern. Sometimes it's every day for a week, and then we go weeks without seeing one another. It just depends on if she feels like hiding her addiction, and if I feel like pretending, I don't know. The problem is, I've endured and remembered so much of our past together that now my tolerance is short-lived with her. Experience has conditioned me to notice every one of her *addict moves*, and instantly, I become irritated. At thirty-five years old, it's embarrassing to have an addict for a mom. I pray daily for God to release my past hurt so I can see the good in her- to build a better relationship. I know I must forgive her and accept her for who she is, but I struggle with that. Over the years, God has shown me that people can change- He changed me. And because of that, I desire more for her; more for us. I've never understood the euphoria that comes with drug usage, so I can never put myself in her shoes. I honestly don't want to understand; I just want to accept and genuinely love her for who she is. I love her because she's my mom. And I know she has tried to be the best she knew how to be, but I hate what she is, an addict.

My message to me is simple: Hey Alice, you are not your mom; you are YOU. You are pure. You are bold and strong, and God is with you no matter what.

When I see my mom or think about her, I reflect on the goodness of the Lord. I'm reminded that we all have a purpose. Her just being her made me who I am. Her lack of morals made me more genuine. The things she did not do taught me who I needed to be. God placed everyone in my life for a reason. And He chose her to create the fearfully and wonderfully made - me. Thank you, God. Thank you, Mom.

I express to people all the time - you can only be you. Don't let what you've endured or lacked to determine who you are. When life gets overwhelming, and it does, just reset. STOP and LET GO. Battles only weigh you down when they're not your battles. Timing is key. You must know when to trust God. Psalm 37:5 (NIV), *"Commit your way to the Lord, Trust in him and He will do this…"* Keep your eyes focused on your faith and believe everything else will follow.

My favorite quote is, "Greater is Coming." I always believe there's still more in store. We will never reach the pinnacles of perfection God established, so there is always greater to come! I genuinely feel if you always believe there's more than you will reach and strive for.

I have a few questions for you to consider.

Is holding on to painful memories helping you?

Picture yourself in the future-what do you see?

Would you want your kids to forgive you in 5, 10, 15 years from now?

Trauma Ain't Normal™!

DONNA MARIE

Coach Donna Rojas has been actively engaged on the front lines of the offender population for many years. As a certified Offender Workforce Development Specialist (OWDS) and National Global Career Development Facilitator (GCDF), Coach Rojas works directly with the inmate population and facilitates their ability to recognize their strengths, maximize their potential, and achieve marketable outcomes through discipline and positive reinforcements. She continues to develop partnerships with various community and faith-based organizations that provide resources to Justice Involved Women. In the community, she serves as a Commissioner for the Montgomery County Commission for Women and serves as the liaison and advisor for their newly formed "Women's Reentry Program."

Coach Rojas' mission is to serve, empower, and motivate returning citizens for successful reentry into *our* community.

Does she even like me? I asked myself this question for many years. As my mom's only child, I felt like an outsider looking in. Maybe it had something to do with the fact that she sent me on a visit that lasted 15 years. My grandmother raised me in the United States Virgin Islands, while my mom pursued her college degree and career in New York City. The next time I lived with my mother, I was 16 years old and a senior in high school. The mother and daughter bond that I yearned for never developed because it seemed like my mother was available for everyone else but me. While she always provided for me financially, the emotional connection was lost, and we struggled. Our rapport was so fractured that I started developing feelings of hatred towards her.

Because of our toxic relationship, my association with others struggled as well. I was so combative. I sought affection and security, and sometimes I struggled to understand why and wondered what was wrong with me. I indulged in some very destructive behaviors, which included smoking weed, popping pills, and trying to fit in. However, I was really trying to fill the gap in my soul that was longing for my mother's love. I could not understand why I didn't have the only thing in life that I wanted the most…a connection with my mom like the ones my friends said they had with their mothers. All I had with her was fight after fight, battle after battle.

One such battle occurred when my mother asked me to wait at home for my cousin. He had something for my mom from my aunt (her sister) and would be at our house around 3:00 pm. Two and a half hours later he hadn't arrived, so I went outside to the nearby park. I kept looking for him while I hung out with my friends, but he never showed up. When I got back in the house, I called my mother and told her that he hadn't come by with the package. So, she called my aunt to see what had happened. About five minutes later, the phone rang, and all I heard was my mother yelling, "Didn't I tell you to stay at the apartment until your cousin came?" I guess I had missed him somehow, and I tried explaining that. We got off the phone, and I thought it was over, but it wasn't. When she got home around midnight, I heard her walking towards my room. Next, the light popped on, and she started in on me. "Didn't I tell you to wait for Allen to bring me something from your aunt?" Sitting up a little, I said in a forceful tone, "I told you before, he never came!" She responded, "Who do you think you are talking to?" and suddenly, I was being pulled out of the bed by my hair. When I regained my footing, I pushed her and screamed, "Get off of me." I kept pushing her, and she started throwing punches at me like we were in a boxing match. We moved from my bedroom into the nearby bathroom. I tried to protect my face, and awkwardly fell right into the tub. I don't know if she was tired or noticed that I was no longer standing, but the battle ended, and she walked out. I waited a minute or two before I moved. Then I got out of the tub, went back to my room, and closed the door. I wanted to slam it because I was so angry, but I didn't want to provoke her anymore. I sat on my bed; I knew deep down inside that what had happened between us was not normal and wondered what made a mother and daughter behave this way. I laid down, and as the tears fell, I went to sleep. After not speaking for a few days, I overheard her on the phone talking, "This child is not like me. She's like her grandmother." When I heard her, I got so mad because my loyalty to my grandmother was like no other. It was my grandmother, not my mother, that showed me how to love. She was the one that taught me how to pray and see the best in people. My grandmother, in my eyes, did no wrong. How dare my mother talk about her like that?

Months later, after graduating from high school, there was another bad argument, and I had it. That evening I grabbed a handful of garbage bags and began chucking my clothes and all my belongings into the bags. I went to my mother's room and exclaimed, "I'm moving out!" She did not respond. I had a boyfriend named Marvin that lived in the same building, so I moved in with him, his mom, and his younger brother. Mom and I saw each other often inside and outside of the building, and we didn't utter a word to each other. People who knew us would look around in bewilderment.

I was so done with her, yet I couldn't believe I left having my own room with food accessible at any time, to sleep on the floor with my boyfriend, who eventually became my abuser. I remember the first time he hit me, and after he profusely apologized, I said to myself, *hitting must be a part of love.*

My mother and I began speaking again when I shared with her that I was pregnant. She was excited about having her first grandchild but still never expressed the emotions that I wanted her to show towards me. On December 25, 1984, I gave birth to my beautiful daughter. Afterwards, my mother and daughter's father left to celebrate Christmas with other family members and friends. I sat alone in a hospital room feeling even more disconnected from my mother and hoped that I would not treat my daughter the same way. However, years later, I repeated painful behaviors I had with my mom, with my daughter. This included sending my baby to live with the grandmother who raised me. My daughter didn't return to live with me until she was nine years old.

When my daughter reached high school age, I figured it was time for me to enjoy living my life. My daughter watched my son while I hung out with friends. At home, I was a disciplinarian and hard on my daughter yet overprotective with my son. Like my mom did me, I too kept pushing and pushing my daughter until she and I were about to have an all-out fight. I sarcastically commented on her affiliation with her friends and their parents. I criticized her for how accepting she was of them while treating me like an outsider. They knew more about her than I did. By now, she was a college-aged young adult, and a discussion we had escalated, and she screamed, "Mom, you are such a b....." At that moment, her words hit me hard. I had felt the same way about my mom. Something needed to be done, but I did not know what that was. I just knew that I was the adult and my attitude was that I didn't need to change anything. But everything around me was changing. By now, my daughter left home to live on her own, and my son was about to graduate from high school.

I admit, I have struggled with being overbearing with both of my children. I know I was critical of them and their actions. At times I have been guilty of favoring one over the other. My mindset and behavior emulated my mother, and that needed to change. I was still yearning to be accepted by my mother. I was constantly challenged with not receiving the love and attention while growing up, and now my attitude and behavior had trickled down to my children. I had to stop another generation from being affected.

Forgiveness was the only option for me; it had to happen because I was so angry on the inside. I went to church one Sunday and heard a teaching on forgiveness. The pastor taught from the section of the Lord's Prayer, which says, "And forgive us our debts, As we forgive our debtors." Matt 6:12 (NKJV) If I wanted forgiveness for the things that I had done, I had to forgive first. And the people on the top of my list to forgive (besides myself) was my mother and my abuser. Even after that sermon, I went through many peaks and valleys as I began to deal with my insecurities. I had to finally come to grips with the fact that I had to rely on someone bigger than any human; I had to trust in God. I got down on my knees, and through the tears, I prayed in earnest. *God, please help me. Help me to forgive myself for the things I've done and to forgive those who I feel have done wrong to me. God, please touch my mother's heart right now. I cannot stand the way she treats me, and she does not understand how I feel. She doesn't see anything wrong with how she is, and when I talk to her about it, she doesn't even apologize. She has hurt me in ways that may not matter to her, but I have to let this go because it is affecting how I interact with my children.* I had a real conversation with God. As I got up, I wiped the tears and left my hurt and pain with God.

I now know the only person who I was responsible for when it came to my mom and me was me. I had to be accountable for my actions and reactions. I was the one who was liable for the way I responded. I needed to be more assertive and not so aggressive. When I allowed myself to get rid of the hurt and stopped repeating unhappy memories in my mind, I finally had a release within my spirit and truly became free. I apologized to both of my adult children, close friends, and family who were victims of my aggressive behavior and our associations have now improved. One scripture that stayed with me through everything was Psalm 121:1-2 (NKJV), *"I will lift up mine eyes unto the hills, from whence cometh my help. My help cometh from the LORD, which made heaven and Earth."* I had to learn that no matter how my mother made me feel – I matter, and I am relevant and in times of trouble and concern that I needed to look to God.

One day, I gathered enough courage and had a conversation with her. It was hard, but it was time. She didn't really hear what I was saying, and the call ended with me feeling frustrated and wondering, *why do I keep trying with her?* But I was able to share with her something that hurt me for a long time, and that was her hiring and accepting a man who had abused me. Moving forward, I know I am in control and that I should not give anyone the ability to control my emotions, especially my mother.

Through the years, to deal with my momma trauma, I have learned my triggers and have developed mechanisms to keep them at bay. There are still times when she'll say things that may trigger negative emotions and memories that cause me to feel low, but how we engage each other and what things in my life I will give energy to – I decide those things.

In my past, I allowed criticism, personal attacks, and rejection to define me as a person, but I didn't know any better. Now I know that I am important. I am beautiful and that I was created for a reason. God chose my parents as the conduit for me to do great work on Earth, and the Bible is a good reminder that God uses the most unsuspecting characters to bring out His purpose. One of my cousins helped me to understand that people show love in different ways. I often wonder about the experiences my mother had that caused her to act the way she did towards me. All I wanted, my entire life, was a relationship with my mother. One filled with love, hugs, admiration, and an emotional connection. However, it came to a point where I knew that my Heavenly Father was all I really needed. I had to understand my mom would not change or at least in the way that I needed. Modest improvements were clear once I let the negativity and feelings of woundedness go. In the forefront of my mind, I focused on the good things about her. I now choose how to engage, and my main goal with her and others is to maintain peace. I'm proud to say we are now in a better place, and no matter what, I have always and still love her dearly.

What I want to share most about my life with you is that you cannot allow the behavior of others to dictate who you are or who you will become. If you have experienced similar trauma to mine - do not let what transpired to define you as a woman.

Life is about learning and being authentic in who we were created to be. Motherhood doesn't come with a manual. We must take what is beneficial from our mother's and implement those things that are of value. However, we must try to make sure that we do not make the same mistakes with our children.

If you have been scared by your relationship with your mother, please do whatever needs to be done to heal, even if it means getting help.

We cannot allow ourselves to succumb to those negative episodes because if we do, the cycle will never end.

I decided to get spiritual and mental help because I wanted to be free from the hurt that I had held on to. Because of my trials and successes, I can now share with the women who I coach, who are a part of the criminal justice system, how I made it through those tough times with my mom. I am building a brand that empowers women not to be defined by their inmate number or what they have gone through. Instead, they, too, can succeed and reenter society trauma-free.

Three questions, I would like to ask you to think about are:

If your momma doesn't change, what will you do?

When triggered by your momma, how will you react?

What tangible steps will you take to move past what your momma has done?

Trauma Ain't Normal™!

AMIRA MICHELE

Amira Michele Management (AMA) was founded by Amira Bethea, a native of Brooklyn, NY, who now lives in Portsmouth, VA. Amira's love for music started at a young age to escape from the harsh growing pains of the African American struggle. Music was her inner peace, her therapy, and her escape to freedom. Being in the midst of the evolution of hip-hop, and also in the state of New York, Amira had a musical advantage, and her ear for talent had emerged, although unknown at the time, she would eventually move forward towards her purpose. Amira is a co-author of the book, *Gotta Story To Tell.* She is also a mother of three and in a relationship with Lakeesha *Klu* Atkinson. She serves as Co-Chair to Believe.Pray.Overcome, a non-profit that supports other organizations through ribbon T-shirt campaign sales to raise funds for their causes. She also serves on the Board of the MAN (Men Alleviating Negativity) Foundation as a fundraising chair. It is evident that Amira is a natural-born leader, and the road to success in the future is promising for a woman of her expertise, knowledge, leadership, and love with a passion for giving back.

Trembling on the toilet seat as bright red blood flowed from my tiny body, I yelled, "Mother, mother, come here; please hurry!" Ten minutes later, Mother came down the long hallway. "What do you want, and why the hell are you yelling?" Tears flowed down my chunky cheeks. "I'm bleeding, and it won't stop." She handed me a long, white pad. "Here bitch, take this and put it on. You'll be fine." When she left the room, I felt my soul leave me that day. I wiped my tears, cleaned myself the best way I knew how, and placed the menstrual pad between my legs. And from that day forward, I knew that she would not be what I needed her to be...ever.

Through the years, Mom had so many times to redeem herself, and yet, repeatedly, she has failed me. When two fingers were shoved into me, she wasn't there as I cried out her name. Lying on my molester's bed victimized and helpless, I kept asking myself, *why me?* I was a little girl at the age of nine whose innocence was stolen without a care in the world. All alone, I had to go through that by myself. I believed my molester when he told me my mom was not in her right mind and that if I told what he had done, she wouldn't believe me, anyway. That day or any other, she wasn't there to give me a tight bear hug or let me know that I'd be okay. Even when I became a teenager, again, she wasn't there to wipe the tears from my eyes and tell me a situation with a boy wasn't right at all. She didn't even say I had a choice on who I let in my body.

Constantly I try to think about any happy memory that I have with her, and there aren't too many. One time when we were living in Brooklyn, New York, she picked my brother and me up from our aunt's house (my father's sister). My father was absent, too, doing whatever he wanted. Mother didn't come around much due to her being on drugs, so when she did, we were so happy because at least we would get a good, hearty meal. Those types of meals were slim to none at our aunt's crib. When Mother arrived, we ran down three flights of stairs in my Nana's brownstone to get to her. We tried jumping in her arms, but she wouldn't have that. She looked well mostly if I hadn't noticed the mascara pieces stuck to her lashes and her brittle lips, but her clothes were clean. With brother on one side and me on the other, she grabbed our hands, and we walked to where mother was staying.

We saw so many people and mother was very popular. Some men we passed yelled out and asked, "We gone see you tonight?" She hollered back, "Don't you see me with my damn kids!" I knew why mother was pissed, and what the guy referred to. He was the same dude I saw her with at the neighborhood crack house. I saw mother do some things with this man that were so nasty. I wished she didn't have to do such things, but she did what she had to do to feed her habit. At Mom's, she made us chicken, rice, and cabbage, and it was so good. Mother knew how to cook, and she never lost that touch. We ate and watched television. A commercial came on and posed a question, "What do you want to be when you grow up?" My brother replied, "A drug dealer."

Mother screamed at the top of her lungs, "No, the hell you don't!" It was the first time that I saw mother get so angry, but it wouldn't be the last. Eventually, my mom and dad got back together and moved us to Virginia.

A memory I've tried to blackout was when my mom had just finished cooking chicken noodle soup. After eating, I walked back into the kitchen to put away my dish. Mom was finishing up washing the other dishes in the sink. I politely slide my bowl and spoon into the soapy water. And when I did, something didn't feel right – I felt her rage. She looked deep into my soul and said, "You little bitch, daddy's girl. You think you can get away with everything." I didn't understand where all of her anger was coming from. My intentions were pure. *Me placing dishes in a sink got you this mad?* I thought. I walked away with no argument or response. Then suddenly, I felt wet, soapy hands wrapped around my neck. The pace of my breathing became heavy, and the thought of me fighting for my life hovered over me. The lady I hated to call my mother was letting me know that she would kill me with no regrets. My savior, my pop's, yelled, "Hey, what the hell is going on in there?" Mom released her grip. I sighed in relief and swallowed every bit of air around me. All I could think about was me and the bundle that grew in my belly. "Get out of my face, daddy's girl!" Mother screamed. I ran out of the kitchen and past my pop's. "You okay?" I ignored him, grabbed my car keys, and went for a ride. A puddle of tears rested in my lap, and 'til this day, I can't figure out what I did to mother for her to treat me that way. I didn't ask to be in this world, so why didn't she just close her legs so she wouldn't have to worry about even having me?

I can't fault mother to a certain point, I guess, because of how she was raised and the many traumatic situations she encountered before and after me. Going from a child, teenager, college student, wife, mother, and then to a crack head had to be the hardest life trail to walk. Her life reminds me of the book, "The Coldest Winter Ever." The book hits home because of mom's situation and what she went through. My life is kind of like it, too. My mother was not there that much for me, and my father was absent when I was younger. Do I feel sorry for her? In the past, I did, but now, I no longer can because adults have to make adult decisions. I blame her a lot when it comes to me becoming a woman. Mother never told me how beautiful I was. Looking in the mirror, trying to build my confidence due to never receiving it was hard. Yes, I think I am the shit, but the lacking of confidence was there. Mother always was envious of me, and to this day, I don't know why. Mother never fully walked me into womanhood. Her only theory was let no one disrespect you more than once. I guess that explains why I was in so many fights when I was a teenager. No matter what, though, I listened to mother regardless of the level of respect I had for her.

At this point in my life, I'm deciding to walk this path without her. I have a guy I am in love with, and I really think that we may not be a forever ever kind of thing, but I am seven months pregnant and weigh two hundred and two pounds. He's the father and currently incarcerated. Being pregnant is one thing, but doing it alone is another? I am afraid for my unborn child. Here I am with an unborn child kicking me daily to let me know he is ready to be in this cruel world. I have no clue what to do with him once he gets here. I can't extend my love to him because I don't have it in me right now. How do I love? What the hell is love? My mother was never a mother. She was selfish, and my greatest fear is that I'll continue the cycle- at least that's what it feels like now.

And every chance mother gets, she reminds me that my boyfriend/son's father didn't care enough to be around me. He told me otherwise, but was mother telling the truth? Being pregnant has me wanting to try to forgive mother for all she has put me through, but my heart has no more room for heartache.

But I'd rather make millions of mistakes with my soon to be born son instead of letting her come back into my life and corrupt my state of being. I have to learn on my own, and I have to stand on my own two feet. I am grateful for my sister, but she has done enough trying to fulfill mother's place. It's time for her to let me go and to learn as well. Wow, the journey of motherhood is coming my way, and there's no manual for me. But guess what? I have my faith, my state of mind, and the blood flow running from my heart to make this work. My son will heal my broken hurt from everything, and for that, I will be forever grateful. At this moment, he is what matters the most, and I know I can't let him down. As his mother, I am aware of that, and I will be there no matter what it takes. I thank my mother for birthing me and for giving me the opportunity to show my son what a mother is supposed to be. With her still living and our relationship not being what it needs to be, I do thank mother for her presence, to remind me of what to become. I always hope that we could get to a better place because I crave for the mother and daughter relationship every single second of my life. The little girl in me still cries out on the inside for the comfort of my mother's love. Mother will never understand what her decisions have done to me. But mother will see what her choices have turned me into. I am a low tolerance female that will continue to mend her broken heart while conquering every trial and tribulation that comes her way.

But the question will always remain, *"Why my mom?"*

Trauma Ain't Normal™!

YOLANDA MYRICK

My businesses Great Things Christian Childcare Center and GREAT Consulting Firm LLC., are personal. Sixteen years ago, when we moved from New York to Virginia, we needed childcare. We settled on a pretty corporate facility. We had no idea how badly they would under-serve our super-active busy-bee baby until a phone call. Our baby had fallen and hit her head on the ground. But it wasn't just a fall. It was an act of neglect that was detailed and sadly recorded in court documents that the young lady in charge of protecting her, simply didn't care. It was in the emergency room while I waited for the results of our daughter's MRI that I received the clearest vision of Great Things Christian Childcare Center.

It is not business when I enroll a child. I become that mother all over again but in the most purpose-filled way. When I hire a team member, I am that mother all over again but in the most intentional way. It's not enough to just love children to work in this industry - I train my staff to be aware of the importance of serving the social and emotional needs of children and often, their parents as well.

Growing up, I had two working, married parents who absolutely adored me. My mom worked at night and was home during the day to cook dinner, spend time with my sister and me, and do other household chores. She was a loving, faithful wife and took pride in being our mother. However, it all changed as I got older when I witnessed firsthand her domestic abuse, both physically and verbally, by my father. I'm sure their relationship was a determining factor in her suffering from alcoholism. Slowly she began attempting to distance herself from him by not being home as often. She used the excuse saying she was with a friend, but my mom's continued absence led to my intense feelings of abandonment.

Then at 11, I suffered a violent sexual attack in our apartment as I arrived home from school. The intruder had pushed his way into the door. I barely felt my feet hit the floor as I ran down the long hallway to my parent's bedroom door. I just knew she would be there to save and protect me. But she wasn't. After I listened intently for the front door to close, I cried aloud for help – my tiny sized hands were tied behind my back. I felt blood trickling down the insides of my thighs. The timing couldn't have been any worse. My grandmother (her mother) had suffered a heart attack and was in critical condition at the hospital. Because the two of them were so close, I knew my news would affect her. It was my hope she'd come home to my sister and I. My grandmother died a few days later, but that wasn't the only death that occurred. My mother was devastated and hopeless as she lost her best friend while I lost mine.

Daily, I lived in fear. And my feelings that I had been unprotected by my mother swelled. I wanted, no, I needed her to be around. So, to help facilitate and not add to her hurt, I tried especially hard not to burden her. Especially about my conflicting emotions. It was important to me that my family was proud of me, so I held my true feelings deep down within me. Overhearing one of my mom's conversations with her cousin, I found out that she was leaving — not just me in New York, but the state. Mom moved to New Jersey. I stayed with family members. Specifically, my mother's youngest sister. She was the fun aunt with no children of her own. I went from an alcoholic mother who refused to remain sober to an aunt who had mental illness and drug abuse. After evictions, loss of a city job, and a relationship with her kids, I couldn't wrap my mind around the fact that my mom could not remain sober. Living with my aunt, her issues helped to ignore the fact that I had become a rebellious and promiscuous teenager. I had a knack for being in the wrong places at the wrong times. She aided me in being defiant and told my mother I could stay with her while she got settled.

I became a mother for the first time at 24. The father was someone I had been with as a teenager. Never wanting my child to feel what I did, abandoned and unprotected, I overcompensated out of fear. Even with my low self-esteem, I did whatever was necessary to provide for my son. I asked no one for help. I had to; when his father was incarcerated, I became a single parent. Even now, I have to check myself occasionally. I struggle with being a good mother. I'm quite protective of how others treat my kids, and I feel the need to safeguard their emotional stability – even when there is no serious threat. I admit, my actions have had negative effects on my husband and kids. But again, I self-correct, and my husband knows of the root cause. He steps in and helps me emotionally recalibrate.

Although my mother is no longer here, I love her. I remember her as she was; loving, caring, and so giving. As an adult, I can now emphasize with her struggles and her pain. It had to be a lot. The problem was getting myself to understand she would never be able to make up for the lost time. I knew it was not my job to judge her but to forgive her. My road to forgiveness was to use each day to renew my expectations and to remind myself that none of us has forever on Earth. I try to remember that I am not perfect, and that love covers a multitude of sins. I desire to have the best memories of my mom as possible. She supported me the best way she could, and

I've matured to accept that. Disappointment still lingers because, as her little girl, I didn't have her attention and support as I wanted. But I totally forgive her.

My mom and grandmother left me with a good foundation, and though our lives were not perfect - they instilled in me solid Christian values. Deep in darkness, some days, I felt that no one would miss my presence from this Earth. It was God's love that gave me the strength to want to see another day to become a better person, and I knew I had to keep going. But I got my will to live from my mother and allowed God, my father, to save me from death. I survived depression and bouts of anxiety because I knew my family did not want to see me go out that way. I remember how much family meant to my grandmother and mother before life got in their way.

Hi Yolanda. Your mommy always loved you. God sees all things and has not forgotten about you. No matter how painful it feels to be without the perfect mommy, you don't have to live in anger and regret. You can change the pattern but in a healthy and productive way.

To the one reading my story: Take one day at a time and remember you have the right to feel how you do. You were not wrong. If the thoughts and memories of bad times get you down, it's okay to take a break, come back to it and try again. But please do not hold in the pain of your past and don't say, "I'm ok," when you know you are not. Your life matters because your time on this Earth is limited and it is meant for you to live it to the fullest. If you begin to feel helpless and overwhelmed by pain, start the process of grieving the mother you wanted to have. What I mean is, let go of the idea of her and understand that particular mom doesn't exist anymore. Instead, find positive ways to see yourself and create positive moments without the expectation of anything in return, including an apology. Get to know the mother you have in front of you if she is still alive. Make new, happy memories with her. You have a voice! So please find that person who creates a safe place for you and speak up. This person can be your spiritual leader, a close friend, and a spouse. Speaking to a professional about your trauma will also help you find peace. Talking about what you have experienced will allow you to vent and feel listened to. Allowing yourself to feel your emotions makes you less ashamed of them. Whether it's yelling or simply needing somewhere to go, avail yourself to go to a safe space and connect with someone supportive, nurturing, and that provides a refuge.

My favorite scripture is 1 John 4:4 (KJV), *"Greater is He that is in you, than he that is in the world."* It reminds me to dig deep and to remember the wonderful things I am created to do and to be. This means discovering a passion or gift you may have and exploring it. It means participating in activities that help bring out your joy and gives you a sense of purpose and fulfillment. The opposite holds true, as well. I heard a message years ago that spoke about when divorce is necessary. The pastor reminded us of the importance of separating ourselves from people, places, and things that negatively affect who we are; our destiny. This way of thinking applies to the adverse behaviors of our mothers who have not yet dealt with their own pain.

I have a few questions for you:

1. How long ago did the trauma occur? This is important to help determine processing time. For example, something recent may be too fresh to deal with, while something that happened long ago may have been buried for a reason.

2. Are you ready to move forward? If not, do you know why? These questions will help you to uncover more underlying issues or identify all parties in the trauma.

3. Is it more important to you that the trauma is acknowledged, or is your peace the most important to you?

SHANNA THOMAS

I have been a professional licensed cosmetologist and make-up artist for the past 26 years in Norfolk, Virginia. I am the owner of Salon Sophistique, where I help bring forth one's inner beauty by enhancing their outer appearance so they can feel more confident and look their absolute best. I know what it's like to let circumstances of life weigh you down and make you feel like you don't matter. We look to others for approval and happiness, and at the end of the day, we need to look within. We have to EMPOWER one another, and that's what I do as often as I can in the salon and out in the world. Salon Sophistique "Where Class meets Sass."

Where did these freckles come from, and how come I don't look like my siblings? Everyone is light-skinned, and I'm darker, were my thoughts as I looked in a mirror.

The story told to me was that my father left when I was two years old. My mother said he was a recruiter in the army reserves and was from Chicago, his father owned a funeral home and he was married. As I grew older, my questions got more solid, and my mother was not too happy when I asked about him. She answered my questions to the best of her ability (so I thought), but I could tell in her tone that she didn't want to answer me. Her irritation was undeniable when I saw my mom's folded arms, and her quick mood change was so obvious. I hated how dismissed she made me feel. I had a right to know who and where my father was. For my mother to act as if I bothered her when I asked her specific things just broke my heart. Her responses made me believe I was unwanted even the more. I thought their split was my fault and that I was the reason he skipped out on me. I can recall at five years old asking, "Can we call my dad?" I was so excited and anxious. Mom called him at work only to be told, he didn't work at that job anymore. I was so let down. It seemed like for my entire childhood, I felt alone and abandoned. *Why didn't he love me? What did I do? How could he leave his own flesh and blood?*

As I grew older, the attention I received from boys made me feel wanted and special. Since my own dad didn't want me, somebody out there would. I associated love as sex. And when I had sex, to me, that meant the person loved me. So, I hunted for love in a lot of empty places. I was also molested by one of my mother's now-deceased brothers. I escaped an attempted rape just to be actually raped later on. These traumatic things led to my promiscuity and fueled the desire I had to be loved in ways I thought were normal.

My uncle, a retired U.S. Marshall (not the uncle who molested me), offered to help me find my dad, but only when I thought I was ready. And when I turned thirty-seven, I decided I was ready and had a conversation with my mom about it.

"I want to find my father," I said as a thirty-pound weight seemed to lift from my soul.

"Find your father? He's down here." Mom said matter-of-factly.

I couldn't believe what I heard because my mother never told me where he lived. N.E.V.E.R. I raised my voice at her, "What do you mean he is down here? Down here, where?"

"We left Philadelphia in '92 and moved to Virginia."

In my head, I repeated her words, *here in Virginia?* "Whatchoo mean?" I finally said aloud.

The look on my mother's face was like a deer caught in headlights. I could tell she realized she had said too much when she started playing her Nintendo DS without any direct eye contact with me. She shrugged her shoulders and repeated her words, "He's down here somewhere, I don't know."

I remember leaving her room, certain that she never told me where my daddy lived. I realized she had slipped up and hadn't meant to give up those details. I left the house and got in my car, and I lost it. I felt betrayed. After all these years, how in the world did she think I would've been okay? She said it so matter of fact like. As if what she said wouldn't make me have more questions. She knew I had been longing to find out who and where he was. I had two important questions for her, but it wasn't about my father. 1. Why has she been lying to me? 2. What more is she keeping from me?

As a cancer survivor, I decided to actively search for my father for several reasons. The first was I desired closure. Second, I needed more information concerning my family medical history and third because, as a single, divorced woman, I didn't want to end up dating my uncle's cousin brother. And the bonus reasons were my daughters- I had them to think about as well. Right away, however, there were two major problems I found with the search criteria I entered. There was a possibility the name my mother gave for my father was false. Problem number two was the man that molested me, my mother's brother (my uncle) might be my father. When I asked my mother about that being a possibility, she stated, "Not that I know of."

Huh? Not that you know of? You gotta be kidding me, man!

I prayed that Jesus would take the wheel. Let me be honest cuz asking Jesus to take tha wheel sounded real good, but in all actuality, I was cussing up a storm, infuriated and bewildered all at the same time. My life had to have been some kind of horror movie or a bad dream that I just couldn't wake up from.

This newfound information made me not even want to trust my own mother. I felt bamboozled and adrift more than ever. I have bouts with anxiety, depression, anger issues, self-love, and worth were at a low. I keep to myself, and I deal with things on my own. I'm angry most of all because my mother knows the truth, but she will not tell me. That hurts like HELL. I don't even have the words to express how I feel inside. It's hard for me to function some days. I smile and act normal, but deep down, I am a hot mess. Even though I am a stylist and my artistic expression flows through my hair, make-up, and style of dress; It's easy for me to mask and bury all the hurtful situations- that come naturally to me. I thought I was loving myself, but, in all actuality, I was running, hiding, ducking and dodging. We all have a right to know where we come from. It's time out for the lies and the sweeping things under the rug. My mother said that her experiences with my father were extremely painful, and she does not want to discuss it. It is my hope, one day, mother would get released and healed from all of the trauma that happened in her own life.

Before my mother's slip up, our relationship was good. But now, I barely want to be around her. She will be eighty soon and no longer drives. I take her to her doctor's appointments and wherever else she needs to go. It's tough because when I look at her, all I want to say is, "Momma, I want the truth, and you won't even give me that. Here I am serving you, and I can't get this one thing? How unfair is that?"

I realize now that she has her own pain, and I pray one day I will forgive her for knowingly and unknowingly bleeding on me from her traumatic wounds. Right now, forgiveness for me seems impossible to reach because my mother knows how important finding my father is to me. For the life of me, I don't understand how her demeanor is so nonchalant when I ask her about different things. A mother should want to help their child and to know she won't break my heart. With all honesty, I want to take her to the streets and fight her! But that wouldn't solve a daggon thang.

In order to truly forgive her, and I want to, I have to get this anger off of me by dealing with my past. Whenever she asks me to do anything, I cringe. I get an attitude and not wanting to do anything she asks of me, but I suck it up and do it for her because no matter what the truth is, she is my parent, and I have to honor her even though in my eyes she doesn't deserve it.

If I could go back and give the little girl in me advice, I would tell her... Your father leaving you was not your

119

fault, and parents aren't perfect. No one is, for that matter. You are beautiful. You are loved. You are not less than because your father wasn't in your life. Mothers aren't perfect, and they do the best they know how to do, so don't hold things against her. Get to know God so that you can know true love. And most of all that little girl needs to know, you are enough, and don't you ever forget that!

To those with their own momma trauma, I advise you to seek help. Go to a counselor, talk about your issues. There will be days where you will fight to smile, shoot, to keep it real you'll fight to get up out the bed. Take those moments for yourself. Give yourself some downtime; just don't stay there long. Go cry even scream if you have too! Going in my car and just shouting at the top of my lungs helps me release anxiety. But keep in mind it's only a temporary fix. Be diligent and open up to someone you can trust- that'll help as well, such as a counselor or a psychiatrist. Let me be real with you, though. In all that I have experienced throughout my life and especially the past year, I turned from God. I would do you a disservice by saying, *oh, just pray about it.* Because when you are hurt and hurting, you ain't thinking about prayer. You may even blame God for all you are facing. But I will say this, I know him, and I'm so glad in my season of (turning away) He has been, and HE is, with me. He never left my side.

"No test or temptation that comes your way is beyond the course of what others have had to face. All you need to remember is that God will never let you down; he'll never let you be pushed past your limit; he'll always be there to help you come through it." 1 Corinthians 10:13 (TM)

For real for real, God will not put more on you than you can bear. I reflect on that thang because even though I'm trying to figure out how in the world can all of this be and why me and I can't make it, that scripture comforts me in knowing I'm strong enough to handle it and if I couldn't, I wouldn't be going through it. So, let that scripture and my story encourage you. Though you may feel alone, you are not; you can make it. You actually are already making it. It's about perspective.

I declare that you will make it through your journey and that you will help so many others just like you who have the same or similar story. Though you may feel you're gonna break, God has His hands on your life. We all have our own race to run, pace yourself, stay focused, keep pushing cause there is someone out there waiting to hear your story so that they can have hope. And last, remember Trauma Ain't Normal, so deal with it. No more sweeping it under the rug or wearing masks trying to hide it. Deal with it head-on. Face it. You got this. Someone is waiting on you to get through and make note, all will happen in God's timing.

Do you let your emotions get the best of you? What strategies can you put in place to help you not go off?

Are you willing to continue in a relationship that has secrets? And at what cost?

Does masking your feelings come naturally to you as it does me?

Trauma Ain't Normal™!

LONEKA WARD

Loneka Tashay Ward is from Portsmouth, VA, and a 2013 graduate of Indian River High School, Chesapeake, VA, where she received an Advanced Diploma. She briefly attended Tidewater Community College studying Fashion Design. She then entered the workforce, where she held several customer service jobs. In December 2016, she reunited and married her 7th-grade sweetheart, Mr. Thomas Ward. To this blended family, they have three children, Brooklynn, Kyree, and Jayce. In 2017 she launched her business 21 Cupcakes. Loneka is a stay at home mom providing love and care for her children while working as a fashion designer in her spare time. She attends Grace Restoration Ministries, Portsmouth, VA, under Pastor Garlena L. Hines. She's active in the Marriage, Women's Ministry, and serves as a greeter.

I don't remember much, but I was told my mom got hooked up with this dude, aka my father, and ever since they met, her life got messed up. My mom had a bad drug habit, and it continued after I was born. She left me with my *dad* for the drugs. They didn't stay together long, so I guess that explained why I lived with my dad and his mom, my grandma. They had a drug house where people were in and out, screaming, cussing, fighting all the time. They would leave me in a room alone while they partied and drank all night. Even when I stayed with his mom, he didn't deal with me much. I guess every man who makes a baby isn't a father.

I also guess that every woman who has a baby isn't a mother. From my dad's, I was sent to live with my aunt. My stay was supposed to be temporary, but Mom was still on drugs and continued to whore around- she had no plans to come back and get me. Even when I would go see her, she was living with some older man, and all they did was cuss and fuss. To where the police came and got me because the environment was so bad. Both of them went to jail. Many times, the family tried to have interventions with her so she could get herself together enough to take care of me, but their attempts all failed. I was only two years old, and I had become a ward of the state. They gave my great aunt permanent custody of me.

My mom, while still drinking and drugging, had two more kids. When she told me, she was having another baby, I remember getting so mad. How could she have another kid when she couldn't even take care of the one she already had? By the time I was eleven, I had had enough and would get so angry on the inside that I refused to be bothered with anyone. And because my understanding of what was going on on the inside of me was limited, my aunt got most of my rage. It was crazy because if it weren't for my aunt, I would never have felt any kind of mother's love – but I still craved love from my birth mother. School was no different. I lashed out there too against my teachers. When people tried to tell me what to do I got even madder. I had and still have a very strong personality that most can't handle.

At 12, I started saving my allowance so I could buy gifts for my four siblings. It felt good to see how much they loved my gifts, but I have to admit it kinda hurt me at the same time. I got nothing from them, but I continued doing it for another two years, even when my mom had two more kids. I eventually stopped because I started feeling unappreciated. With the Christmas tree still up in the living room, my aunt sat beside me and told me my mom had been arrested for robbing an old man at a hotel where she, my siblings, and the father of my two younger siblings stayed. I literally couldn't believe it and thought, *what the hell is this lady thinking?* I had hopes of her getting it together. At that moment, I cried, I got mad, and my emotions were all over the place. How was I supposed to feel? My mom was sent to prison for five years and then probation.

The first time I went to see her in Troy, VA, me and two of my sisters traveled to Richmond with their godfather, who was a long-time friend of my mom. In reality, I believe he was the father of my second sister.

He had a family at home, a wife and a son who was my age. I barely slept the night before. I was nervous and scared, but it was something that I wanted to do and felt strong enough to do. When she sat down, I didn't know what to say, and the time went by so fast. The guard came to get her, and a wave of sadness came over me, knowing she would be confined. In the car ride home, I cried most of the time and I'm not sure why. It wasn't like she had really been in my life for me to be so pressed to want her attention.

Throughout her jail time, we wrote to each other, and she apologized for not being who she was supposed to be. As sincere as she may have been, it gave me no frill of emotion. I was unsure of how to respond because we weren't that close. Since she was not around, I decided that maybe I should get closer to my father. I felt a void and couldn't fill it – I knew something was missing, and I thought it might have been him. So, for my 16th birthday, I decided to invite my father to my birthday event, and true to form he never showed up. I was surprised I felt hurt because he had not been to any of my other birthdays.

My mother served all of her time and was released from prison – which I honestly didn't really give a damn. After months of her being home, we only talked a few times. I did, however, invite her and my father to my high school graduation. It was a big enough moment that I expected both of them not to miss. However, when my mother's sister went to pick him up (he doesn't have a driver's license), he was dead drunk. So, he did not come. He then had the nerve to call me at my graduation dinner, acting as if he wasn't invited, and no one came to pick him up. Like seriously, how could he ruin such a big moment for me? My dad was a loser, then just like he's a loser now.

While I was in the phase of figuring out life as an adult, I moved in with my mom. It seemed okay for a while because, in the beginning, she was more like a friend than a mother. But after having her borrow and asking for so many things (money, using my car), her actions began to annoy me. One day after an argument, we got into a physical altercation, and she tried to bite me. I literally yelled and told her how much I hated her, how much I felt like she won't anything, and how useless she was. The police were called, but no charges were filed. I was just asked to leave. As I was getting my stuff, my siblings started grabbing my things and helped me by throwing them into the street.

A year later, I was pregnant with my first son. I was so excited. My sister-in-law, my brother's wife, gave me a baby shower, and my mother was invited, and my aunt, who raised me, was there. My aunt spoke, and, in her speech, she encouraged me to always respect my mother and thanked my mom for allowing her to raise me. Instead of my mom saying thank you and basking in the moment of her daughter's baby shower, she got upset and felt like she was attacked. My mom was always the victim. In November, I went into labor for about eight hours. I was in tears from so much pain when my mom showed up. In the room, she played close and kind of, in a way, told me to toughen up and then left. Suddenly, me and my sister heard someone yelling "ass hole." I couldn't get up to see who it was because I had an epidural. Apparently, my mom had made such a scene that they had to escort her out of the hospital. I think she was probably hungover or still drunk from the night before. I literally couldn't believe here she was again, messing up another special event for me. After the birth of my son, she did not come to my house when my siblings came to see her first grandson. A few months later, she sent me a message and said what happened at the hospital was not her fault and that my aunt attacked her. Once again, she was the victim. She said my aunt had always kept me away from her, which was a lie. She's just not ready to be my mother.

I was done trying to have a relationship with her. She never takes responsibility; It's always somebody else's fault, and I'm just good without her at this point.

This guy I dated in middle school hit me up. It's crazy because he told me at 12 he would marry me, and there he was again in my life. February 2018, he proposed marriage, and I said, "Yes!" I couldn't believe it because my mom, my mom's sister, and neither of my grandmothers had ever married, but here I was about to have a good husband. When we were discussing our ceremony, the decision had to made whether to invite my mom. Her track record of messing up my birthdays, my baby shower, and the birth of my son was already unforgettable. I didn't want to add my wedding to that list. The thought of my mom coming and looking like a *hood rat* and making a scene scared me to death. So, she wasn't invited, and I was good with my decision.

My mom is alive, and I forgive her, but I don't want a relationship with her. My mom is my biological mom, but my aunt is my mother. She's the person who took care of me and gave me that motherly love. She still gives me that love and support, and she's the best GiGi that my sons could ever have. It would be nice to have a healthy relationship with my mom, and the Bible says for me to honor her, and I do. But the Bible didn't tell me to trust her or let her keep hurting me. One thing for sure, I'm going to work my butt off to make sure this curse in my family is broken, and Kyree and Jayce won't have to one day say like I had to, "why my mom?"

I don't have a favorite song, but I like "I Smile" by Kirk Franklin because I'm learning that if I can keep smiling, I'll be alright. Sometimes I feel like crying and walking away, but I'm not going to do to my boys what my mom did me. So, I smile. I don't have a favorite scripture, but growing up with my aunt, she always liked Psalm 34 (KJV). *"I will bless the Lord at all times, and his praise shall continually be in my mouth."* But for real, I'm not there yet; I still cuss when life gets hard. I have not learned to read scripture when it gets hard. I don't like reading for real, so maybe that's why.

For the young ladies like me, it will be okay if your mom is in jail or left you. Every woman having a baby is not a mom and don't waste time holding grudges or being pissed - it ain't even worth it. My mom had many chances to be in my life, but she always *played the victim,* and that got old. If you have kids, be a better mom than the one you had or don't have kids at all. My two sons are my world, and I'm going to be a great mom, and so can you.

What part of my story propelled you to forgive your mother?

If possible, how would you proceed with having a relationship with your mom?

Pat yourself on the back and describe three things that make you a great mom, sister, aunt, or friend.

PRAYER FOR FORGIVENESS

Heavenly Father, I recognize your sovereignty and I humbly ask that you forgive me of my sins. I repent from any offence, unforgiveness, rage and hostility I have kept in my heart toward my mother. I release her now and I accept your forgiveness in the name of Jesus. I ask Father that you would restore me and build me up in YOU. I ask that an overflow of love would fill my heart where the pain used to be. I ask Father that Holy Spirit would continue to guide me into all truth. I praise you now and forever.

In the matchless name of Jesus, I pray,
Amen.

I'M SORRY

I'm sorry that I'm sorry. I'm sorry for all that I couldn't or wouldn't get right as your mother. And I know you've heard this before but today, this moment, I really need you to hear me not just with your ears but with the remainder pieces of your heart that I didn't break, step on or appreciate.

For every moment I made you feel insecure about your weight or your hair, or your intellect, I'm sorry.

I'm sorry you struggle with "not being enough."

I'm sorry that you now doubt yourself because of me.

I'm sorry your confidence wavered because I didn't teach you how valuable you really are.

For every tear I made you cry, I'm sorry.

For all of those times I screamed and cursed you, I'm sorry.

I'm sorry for all the hateful, mean and spiteful words I said to you.

It's not your fault – it never was – I'm sorry.

For every lie, I'm sorry.

For all those nights you went to bed wondering if I was coming home, I'm sorry.

I could make up so many reasons and justifications for my actions but we're way past that moment, I hurt you, deeply, consistently and without regard, I'm sorry.

I'm sorry for staying down and making excuses when he hit me in front of you.

I'm sorry for every punch, slap and kick you witnessed, especially the ones you took in my place.

I'm sorry for leaving you when you begged me to stay.

I'm sorry for only caring about me.

I'm sorry for not being able to give you what you wanted, what you deserve – a mother that loves you, unconditionally.

I'm sorry for not giving you what I know you've always wanted and that was me…I'm so sorry.

I'm sorry for promises reneged on.

I'm sorry for manipulating you to defer your dreams for mine.

I'm sorry for stealing more than money.

I'm sorry for the questions of others you feel forced to answer because of my foolishness and immaturity.

I'm sorry for the awkward moments, the awkward silence when you see me.

I'm sorry that your heart hurts because of me.

I'm sorry - I'm sorry - I'm sorry - I'm sorry - I'm sorry - I'm sorry - I'm sorry - I'm sorry - I'm sorry - I'm sorry - I'm sorry - I'm sorry - I'm sorry - I'm sorry - I'm sorry - I'm sorry.

A thousand times, I'm sorry.

Please forgive me daughter,

I love you, Momma

"I'm Sorry" Written by Monique Jewell Anderson
Author and Publisher
"Igniting the fire inside You until Your potential becomes Your reality!"
www.SpiritFilledCreations.com

Why My Mom? is pivotal, as women learn that they are not what they were born into. Envision Lead Grow understands the decisions mothers make can impact generations to come. Envision Lead Grow is a 501c3 non-profit on a mission to break the cycle, and transform communities of poverty into communities of promise. Every day, we teach little girls to continue to dream beyond their environment and create their future through entrepreneurship. We offer girls the opportunity to engage with mentoring and training, all at no-cost to them, designed to guide them along the path towards entrepreneurship. Our girl bosses understand they are in control of their futures. 100% of our girl bosses reported planning to graduate high school and attend college. Join us in this transformative work. Get involved in empowering the moms of tomorrow, the women of the future, and the leaders for our next generation.

Visit us at www.envisionleadgrow.org
Facebook: www.facebook.com/EnvisionLeadGrow
Twitter: @EnvisionLeadGro
Instagram: @envisionleadgrow
Dr. Angela's Instagram: @iamdrangreddix
Dr. Angela's Facebook:
www.facebook.com/drangelareddix

Trauma Ain't Normal™!

Made in the USA
Lexington, KY
11 November 2019